Trauma Narrative Treatment
A Trauma Recovery Model for Groups

By: W. David Lane, Ph.D.
Mercer University
Atlanta, Georgia
USA

Donna E. Lane, Ph.D.
Mercer University
Atlanta, Georgia
USA

1

Trauma Narrative Treatment
A Trauma Recovery Model for Groups

It is intended for use by the purchaser and may not be replicated, reprinted, distributed, or used for any other purpose without the express written consent of the authors of the curriculum. All rights are reserved for this material, its printing, copying, use, and distribution.

This model is intended for use with the story, *Gold Stone*, by David and Donna Lane.

Bear's Place Publishing

Lilburn, GA

ISBN-13:978-0692522295

ISBN-10:
0692522298

Dedication

To the people of Haiti:
Romans 5:3-5
Romans 8:28

To Cody, who wrote his story of love and miracles

Table of Contents

Acknowledgements

We are very grateful to all of the people who have been involved in the writing, field testing, and research for the development of these materials. Chief among them, we are thankful for the openness and acceptance of the Haitian people, who were willing to bravely share their own stories with us, as they began the process of preparing to rise from the ashes of their losses. Their resilience is the most powerful symbol of writing a different story for the future that I can think of. It is our sincere hope that these materials continue to impact individuals with hope and healing, inspiring others to share and write their own endings to their stories.

Others who helped immensely:

Sarah Amuka, Brittany Brown, Keith Myers, Stan Hoover, and Auvronette Guilbeaux, Mercer University graduate students who helped immensely with the literature review;

Bloodine Bobb-Semple and Rose Donatien, both Mercer students who traveled to Haiti as part of the training team to do the training workshops for the Haitian volunteers. Both of these wonderful bilingual ladies were Haitian Creole speakers and provided wonderful expertise and boundless energy for the project;

Olivier Clermont, a Haitian native and Mercer graduate student who made every trip to Haiti with me to act as translator and facilitator. This project would not have been possible without Olivier and the graciousness of his family who hosted us for each visit in Port au Prince;

Dr. Kenyon Knapp and Dr. Linda Foster, Mercer faculty members who participated in trips to Haiti and were instrumental in the workshop training sessions;

Dr. Charles Tardieu and the University of Jeremie Project, Jeremie, Haiti: Dr. Tardieu is former Minister of Education for Haiti and was instrumental in arranging meetings with various dignitaries and leaders who helped connect us to groups desiring training. Dr. Tardieu hosted a week long training for 85 teachers in Jeremie, Haiti;

Dr. Joel Dorsinville and the Haitian Baptist Fellowship who carved out time in their annual Haitian Baptist Convention, got us on the agenda for training, and helped facilitate the training for 133 pastors at the Christian University of North Haiti in Cap Haitian, Haiti;

Dr. Rosalie Benjamin and Dr. Ginette Maguet of Institut de Developpement Personnel et Organisationnel (IDEO), Port au Prince, Haiti, who coordinated and hosted a week long training for 21 community volunteers at the IDEO facility. Dr. Benjamin had been tasked by the Haitian Health Ministry to coordinate mental health relief efforts and provided valuable information and linkages to individuals and groups for training and intervention;

The Cooperative Baptist Fellowship, who provided funds and personnel support to carry out the work in Haiti. Special thanks to Dr. Daniel Vestal, Dr. Harry Rowland, and Dr. Reid Doster for their support, friendship, and encouragement;

Dr. Jim Jennings and Conscience International who surprised me one day out of the blue with the idea for the Haiti work, provided funding for the travel and trainings, and who continue to solicit my input and involve me in projects in areas of need throughout the world;

and to Mercer University, a teaching and service oriented university, the likes of which could only be matched, never exceeded.

We know we have left some people and agencies out. Please forgive us. It is our error alone. We hope you know that it goes without saying that we stand on the shoulders of giants.
David and Donna Lane, Atlanta, GA., May 21, 2015

Preface

The genesis of this concept of a group treatment curriculum based on narrative came from the work I did in Haiti after the earthquake in 2010. I was called in early spring, 2010, by Dr. Jim Jennings, CEO of Conscience International, an international, nongovernmental organization that, among other things, provides disaster relief and support in troubled areas around the world. Jim's group had moved immediately on January 10, 2010, in response to the devastating earthquake that left several hundred thousand dead and injured, and approximately four million people displaced. Jim and his volunteers were on the ground in Haiti for the better part of two months working round the clock with the injured and displaced. After the immediate survival needs had been addressed, Jim recognized the extreme need for psychological first aide and trauma care, so he called me.

As founding faculty member and (at the time) Coordinator of the graduate counseling programs at Mercer University, I have been privileged to train hundreds of counselors and to work extensively in the areas of trauma and Post Traumatic Stress Disorder. Jim wanted to put together a program for Haiti to train Haitians to assess and work with the traumatized population. Through the generous funding of the Cooperative Baptist Fellowship and Mercer University, I was able to travel to Haiti to assess the need and meet with key individuals to develop strategies for the most appropriate intervention methods.

In my meetings with Haitian leaders, pastors, and teachers, it quickly became apparent that Haiti has a story-telling culture, and it seemed most appropriate to use narrative based interventions. While still in Haiti I called my wife, Donna, and told her about my idea to develop a narrative group oriented training program with a story as the central focal point of the program. We thought it would be ideal to use actual Haitian history as the story's backdrop. After some initial research on the history and culture of the region, we decided the story would be focused on the trauma to the Arawak culture from the Spaniards landing on Hispaniola. Using figures from Arawak history with whom the Haitian people still identify, along with some other common American and West African symbols to include other elements of the Haitian culture today, we decided on an approach for writing the central story. The next day I called Donna and she informed me the story was ready; that she had prayed about it the night before, and had awakened with the entire story formulated in her mind. It had taken her about four hours to write down what she stated God had given to her as the whole story.

After I came home from that first Haiti trip, with the groups we were to train identified and a plan for the curriculum to train the volunteer trauma workers, Donna and I finalized the story, making it the centerpiece of trauma materials designed to address the issues of psychological first aide, trauma assessment, and group care for trauma victims. We wanted to insure that it was "user friendly" because pastors, teachers, and community volunteers would not be trained therapists and would not have a counseling, psychology, or social sciences background. And so the essence of this curriculum was born.

In three ensuing trips, we were able to train multiple groups of pastors, teachers, and community workers, and assess the efficacy of the materials. The story resonated with the Haitian people with whom we were working, and is still being used today by the over 230 volunteers that we trained. Since then, the Cooperative Baptist Fellowship has funded work in Newtown, CT, using the materials to train pastors and community workers to respond following the Sandy Hook shootings. The story and materials have been used by mission groups in such locations as Cambodia, Malaysia, Jordan, Dominican Republic, Costa Rica, New Zealand, and

China, and in multiple locations across the United States.

Using the Model

This model is intended for use with the story, <u>Gold Stone</u> (2014), by David and Donna Lane, available from Amazon and Barnes and Noble, and from Regeneration Writers Press.

This model is intended for use with small groups, but may be used with individuals as well. The goal of the model is to intervene following a traumatic experience toward preventing the development of severe mental health disorders as a consequence of the trauma experience. It is **NOT** intended for use with people suffering from complex trauma, dissociative disorders, suicidal ideation, or other mental health disorders that make group participation difficult or impossible. These clients should be referred to a mental health professional for a more appropriate level of mental health care.

Introduction

What is your story?

September 11. 2001, New York, Washington, and Pennsylvania, US, terrorist attack; December 26, 2004, India earthquake and Thailand tsunami; August 29, 2005, Louisiana and Mississippi, US, Hurricane Katrina; May 12, 2008, China earthquake; January 12, 2010, Haiti earthquake; March 11, 2011, Japan earthquake and tsunami; April 13. 2013. Boston Marathon bombings, Boston, Massachusetts, US; January 3-7, Nigeria, Baga Massacre; April 25, 2015, Nepal earthquake. This list is just a sampling of traumatic experiences without number that hundreds of thousands have experienced, just in the last fifteen years. Not limited to terror attacks or natural disasters, trauma for individuals takes many forms: witnessing or experiencing violent crimes; rape and/or sexual abuse; physical abuse and domestic violence; the devastation of war and postwar displacement; loss of a loved one; accidents; protracted illness; any circumstance that puts life and limb at risk. These examples of trauma affect almost everyone at some point in their lives. Each day, countless individuals wake up in the morning and the sun is shining, and they feel loved. However, just a short time later, nothing is the same. What do you do when everything you have ever known, everyone you have ever loved, your life as you know it is suddenly changed – wiped away, evaporated, disappeared? Do you quit? Do you run away? Do you decide you want to just die and not face it anymore? Do you even want to go on? Prior to the occurrence of a traumatic event or events, certain basic assumptions guide your life: assumptions like self-determination, basic safety and security, environmental stability, the coming of tomorrow, the presence of the people you love. Then trauma strikes. Suddenly, you are vulnerable and your world is no longer safe and secure. Furthermore, you can't make sense of what is left in the aftermath.

There are many reactions you might have. Initially, you may feel shock, terror, or a sense that what happened is unreal or surreal. You may feel numb, as if you have left your body (a phenomenon called dissociation). Memories might flash before your eyes in horrifying fragments, or you may not even remember all the details (or any of the details) of what just happened. The images of the trauma might replay over and over again, disrupting thought and sleep. New experiences following the trauma may continue to feel depersonalized, meaning they are not connected to you as if you are watching a movie or the experiences are happening to someone else, and your ability to integrate those new experiences into your life story may be compromised. Confronted with the reality of inescapable shock, your mental and bodily systems may begin to break down (Van Der Kolk, 2014).

Many factors impact how you react to a traumatic event: your age (younger persons often react more significantly than older persons); what or who produces the trauma (if a loved one is the agent of traumatic experience, the impact is much more severe); the amount of preparation time you had prior to the event (for example, a hurricane may have several days' notice, while an earthquake has no forewarning); the amount of damage done to you (physically, emotionally, and spiritually) or to your property; the amount of death and devastation you witness; the degree of responsibility you feel for causing or not preventing the event. These are just some of the factors that can impact your reactions to a major traumatic event.

The results of trauma are manifold, including loss of a sense of self, disrupted or fragmented memory, numbing of your depth of feeling with the exception of rage or shame when memory of the trauma is triggered, reorganization of perception where the trauma is superimposed on everything around you, loss of imagination and mental flexibility which impacts coping, immobilization or agitation due to increased secretion of stress hormones resulting in hyper-reactivity to all stimuli, and compromised ability to function socially (Van Der Kolk, 2014).

Loss of Self

One of the initial effects of trauma is a loss of sensory self-awareness. The areas of the brain that work together to create a sense of self, which typically activate when the brain is in "rest" mode, cannot activate because the brain remains constantly activated toward survival of the threat (Van Der Kolk, 2014). At the same time, systems for physical regulation, such as breathing, heartbeat, digestion, hormone secretion, and immunity, become overwhelmed by the perceived sense of threat. You begin to feel disconnected from your own body and mind, and when you lose your sense of your body, you lose your sense of yourself. Knowing what you feel leads to knowing why you feel it which leads to mobilization of resources to manage and respond to those feelings; none of these normal responses occur in the presence of extreme disconnection from the self. As a result, you lose your sense of purpose and direction, the feeling of being alive, and the sense of who you are. You no longer feel in charge of your own life.

Changes in Memory

In the presence of emotionally charged events, you retain an intense memory that is largely accurate, and the more adrenaline is pumped at the moment of the experience, the more accurate the memory is retained, up to a point. However, if the system for storing memory is overwhelmed, such as in the presence of horror and terror, the frontal lobe of the brain shuts down, which interrupts your ability to put feelings into words, breaks down your sense of location and time, stops the flow of information coming into your senses, and prevents proper integration and storage of that information (Van Der Kolk, 2014). As a result, the traumatic experiences are no longer stored as a narrative that is logical, ordered, and understandable; instead, the memories are stored as fragments of sensation and emotion, with little or no story line.

Numbing

The loss of emotional connectivity may be very confusing. At times, you may wonder why you cannot feel the depth of love that you once felt, or the excitement and joy you expect to feel during a special event; however, a sudden onset of deep shame, or a sense of rage that does not appear connected to anything in your present may surprise you. Often, you are not aware of the triggers that stir up the sensations of being in the middle of the traumatic event. It can be something as innocuous as a smell that reminds you of the day of the trauma, or an association with an object that pulls a memory fragment back to the surface. Numbing your emotions may be the response to the intrusion of those memory fragments (Crawford, 2010). Your emotions or lack thereof become a jumble of disconnected messages and sensations that you cannot link as a part of your story.

Superimposition of Trauma

You may have great difficulty deciphering what is going on around you. Intrusive images and sensations make it appear to you that the trauma is happening now (Leahy, 2009). Any stranger walking by on the street may be perceived as a threat. A balloon popping, or a large truck rumbling by on the road, may be heard as a bomb exploding or the beginning of another earthquake. Your spouse walking up behind you may be responded to as something coming to kill you. The smell of supper burning on the stove may cause panic as if the house is burning down around you. Someone touching your arm or tapping you on the shoulder may be perceived as the warning signal for impending abuse. As a result, everywhere you turn is a perceived continued threat to your survival. Your body and mind must remain on alert at all times to deal with the impending danger. The physical and emotional consequences of remaining on high alert are numerous.

Rigidity

Your ability to imagine actually makes problem solving possible. Without your imagination, you are stuck with repeating strategies that have been tried before. Remaining on high alert produces mental rigidity, which results in a loss of imagination and creativity. You may find yourself repeating the same unsuccessful behaviors, even though you are aware those responses did not work in the past, simply because you cannot think of anything else to try. Your brain gets stuck in "ruts" like car tracks on old dirt roads that are dug out by repetitive driving over the same ground day after day. Flexibility, which is a sign of mental health, is lost, and your coping skills are limited. You may even feel compelled to revisit experiences that remind you of the trauma, although it may be terrifying to do so, because your brain is saying you must drive in the "ruts" on the road. At the same time, the brain remains attached to the trauma and is unable to successfully integrate the trauma with new experiences into your life story, resulting in being rigidly stuck in whatever developmental stage in which the trauma occurred. A slow and steady decline in the ability to function in the here-and-now of life is the result.

Agitation or Immobilization

After traumatic experiences, you can become "stuck" in a state of shock. The levels of stress hormones in individuals who have gone through trauma, even well after the experience itself is over, is much higher than normal (Van Der Kolk, 2014). The presence of these hormones leaves you hyper-reactive, sending a signal throughout the body that keeps you feeling agitated, or immobilized, like a bunny cornered in a cave with a wolf at the entrance. You may find yourself in a cyclical response of hyper-arousal followed by hypo-arousal, where you shut down to deal with the overwhelming affective and bodily sensations (Crawford, 2010). The fight-or-flight response is always active. You may erupt unexpectedly over a small, insignificant slight, or you may freeze at the smallest confrontation or disagreement. Either way, your response is out of proportion to the current situation; instead, it is a response appropriate to threat of death.

Impaired Social Function

You are designed to be a social creature. The inability to function adequately in the social context is at the root of multiple mental problems, whether the result of difficulty in creating healthy relationships or the result of problems with self-regulation around others. Because trauma leaves you feelings disconnected from yourself, it also produces a feeling of being out of sync with others. As a result, reciprocity, which is the sense of being seen and heard and known by the people around you, is lost (Van Der Kolk, 2014). If you cannot connect, you cannot function in a group.

The Results of Trauma

The emotional result of trauma is a feeling that everything has been torn apart or lost, including your sense of who you are. Trauma is an external event that tears our lives. There is a pattern to this tearing: memories of the trauma become disconnected and fragmented images and sensations rather than a fluid story with a beginning, a middle, and an ending; the difference between the here-and-now and the past is lost to you, as the trauma invades the present and dictates your responses; you lose your ability to self-regulate and, in a constant state of arousal, you struggle with creating satisfying relationships and functioning in the here-and-now; your sense of self and of being in charge of your own life is lost to you; not knowing what you feel and not knowing why you feel leads to an inability to mobilize your resources to manage life; triggers that remind you of the trauma result in involuntary and repetitive response patterns that recreate the trauma experience but are not connected or appropriate to the present circumstances, leaving you feeling out of control and out of sync with life; ultimately, you feel like an observer of life rather than someone present in it. As Langer (1991) describes it, "Life goes on, but in two temporal directions at once, the future unable to escape the grip of a memory laden with grief." Your experience of the trauma remains separated from your life story, as if it happened to someone else, and disconnected from what you would otherwise experience as a secure and predictable present, dividing your mind in such a way that nothing can seem secure and predictable for you. The trauma itself is unimaginable and unbearable, while day-to-day life goes on. It is as if you are living two lives, the daily experience of the trauma and the daily experiences of working and eating and sleeping and relating in the present. Because you are unable to create meaning from the trauma by integrating it into your life story, that part of yourself is frozen in time.

The ongoing consequences of traumatic experience include feeling heaviness in your chest with difficulty breathing at times, tightening in your throat and holding tension in other areas of your body, remaining on constant alert, experiencing nightmares and flashbacks, disconnecting from self and others, feeling out of control, and staying in a kind of mental "fog" and emotional numbness that makes processing current experiences difficult (Van der Kolk, 2014). In addition, your beliefs about yourself are altered based on the trauma. Self-loathing is common, along with beliefs that you don't matter, are unimportant, have no purpose, deserve what you got, or even are to blame for the trauma happening to you.

Symptoms are not only a normal response to trauma but also a necessary response in order for you to continue to survive. Survival is always the first order of business. But these survival responses to the trauma not only keep you trapped in your pain but also continue the need for the survival responses, creating a self-reinforcing cycle. The unconscious belief becomes, "I need these (feelings/responses/thoughts/behaviors) to survive but these (feelings/responses/thoughts/behaviors) create more unpleasant (feelings/responses/thoughts/behaviors) that make me fear for my survival which creates more of these (feelings/responses/thoughts/behaviors) which makes me believe I need more of these (feelings/responses/thoughts) to survive." Then the emotional trap is complete. You feel fearful or hopeless or overwhelmed or insecure, and more survival response is created. The more you try hard to get over the trauma or deal with it by trying to bury it or change the unpleasant feelings, responses, and thoughts, then the more those feelings, responses, and thoughts are reinforced. This pattern puts an enormous stress on your body and mind. Physical problems, such as autoimmune disorders, heart and blood pressure problems, digestive problems, and chronic fatigue, are often the result. The mind is also overwhelmed, and often shuts down rather than attempting to face the unfathomable. Physical actions create a context for mental activity, but trauma prohibits the appropriate physiological response and successful integration of experiences. You are haunted by bodily sensations and memory fragments that cannot be verbalized, and the body and mind are split as a result (Crawford, 2010).

Symptoms resulting from trauma can include re-experiencing the trauma in the form of nightmares, intrusive thoughts or memories, and flashbacks; disrupted sleep, irritability, exaggerated startled response, and hypervigilance; avoidance of places associated with the trauma, talking about the trauma, or associating with people connected to the trauma; numbing, constriction of emotion, shutting down, and suppression and repression. (Crawford, 2010). What you experience feels as if the past is invading the present, or is still happening in the present.

Survival Responses

Survival responses fall into four general categories:

1. <u>You feel responsible for the traumatic event</u>

   This results from a feeling of having lost all sense of personal power and serves to help you feel a sense of power over the event. Frequently you feel guilt and shame associated with the event. You spend much of your time reviewing the events and trying to anticipate, prepare for, and prevent future trauma.

2. <u>Denial or loss of recollection that the event occurred</u>

   This serves to protect you from dealing with the horrific reality of the event. You may experience a total loss of memory or you may forget significant details of the event. This may last for days, months, or even years. You most likely will recall the trauma at some point, and the memory may be triggered by a random event which may seem unrelated to the event itself. A milder form of denial is a minimization of the severity of the trauma which aids you in continuing to ignore the emotional pain and the torn identity.

3. <u>Aggressive or passive aggressive behavior which results in harm to others</u>

   This group of survival responses is much less socially acceptable and much more harmful. It serves the purpose of taking the focus off of the internal pain and placing it on external objects or people. You want the pain to end but you do not know how to make it stop. Frequently, suicide is not intended to end the *life* but to end the *pain*. You respond to confrontation as an invitation to fight, which seems to bring some relief.

Because of the nature of this type of response it has the potential for permanent damage to self and others.

4. <u>Helping of self and others</u>

This form of survival response has no stigma attached and may not show any outward sign that you are actually attempting to cover internal pain and loss. Instead, most of these responses are applauded and strongly reinforced. You may focus on others' problems so much that you do not seem to have time to deal with your own pain.

The problem with these survival responses is that they serve two opposing purposes. They seem to provide some measure of relief while at the same time reinforcing the problem. Until these patterns become painful or do not work anymore, you will be likely to continue them on an unconscious level. This becomes even more problematic when you have experienced multiple traumas, and if your initial trauma occurred at a very young age.

When Trauma Responses Become Pathological

No one knows why some people seem to manage trauma better than others. Why do some people do OK and some people seem to develop severe problems as a result of trauma? Research has demonstrated that if you develop a secure attachment in earliest childhood, you are better equipped to cope with traumatic experiences (Van der Kolk, 2014). In addition, if you have a strong sense of self, and what is known as an internal locus of control (which means you believe you are in charge of your own life and events in your life are primarily the results of your own actions), prior to the traumatic event, you are likely to handle the trauma better than someone who does not know who they are or someone who believes life happens to them prior to the trauma. These factors also explain, to some extent, why the age you experience the trauma directly impacts how devastating the trauma event will be, with earlier experiences having more destructive impact. Young children have not developed a strong sense of self, and generally still see others (such as parents) or circumstances as in charge of their lives. Finally, if you have a strong social network of support, your chances of managing the trauma successfully are much higher than if you are isolated, or your social network or community is unsupportive or abusive.

All of the responses to trauma that we have discussed are normal survival responses, and most people never develop extraordinary problems. However, most people *do* struggle to cope after trauma and may need some help overcoming the normal responses and difficulties of adjustment associated with traumatic experiencing. This program presents the kind of assistance that addresses those needs. Occasionally, however, responses to trauma can become pathological and develop into psychological disorders that need to be recognized, and the affected people need to be referred to a physician, psychologist, or counselor for further assistance.

Dealing with Trauma

Ordinary memory is basically a story we tell about our lives for a purpose (Van der Kolk, 2014). Our memories are flexible, even changing with retelling, creating a narrative that describes what we have experienced in the context of our whole story. However, traumatic memory is not flexible, not sequential, and serves no purpose, because it is stored as fragments of physical sensations and images, disconnected from language. These memories cannot become part of your overarching story. The effects of trauma are ameliorated when your story can be put into words and shared in an environment of personal safety, so that the memory can be integrated with the emotion, given meaning, included in your life story, and viewed as a past event instead of a present reality (Pack, 2008; Crawford, 2010; Van der Kolk, 2014). Simply talking about the trauma is not enough. First, if described from the disconnected view of someone relaying someone else's story, the memory will not be integrated into your life narrative, and you remain an observer rather than a participant in life. Second, if telling the traumatic event is not connected to the emotion from the event, the inner division described earlier remains intact, leaving you at war with yourself internally (Van der Kolk, 2014). Finally, the rational brain can make sense of emotion, but cannot alter the emotion; in other words, understanding why you feel does not change how you feel (Van der Kolk, 2014). In order to give meaning to the trauma experience, you will need to connect to all aspects of the event, but only in the context of safety and support, having learned the ability to remain connected to mind and body and to have the voice and language to describe the experience with a beginning, a middle, and an ending (Pack, 2008). The trauma story must be integrated into your story, taken beyond memory fragments, sensations, and images into a narrative.

A Research-based Curriculum

This curriculum is designed to be a brief (six session) method for helping people deal with trauma and uses techniques that have been demonstrated through research to be effective. This curriculum uses a story entitled *Gold Stone*, which can be easily shared and relates directly to individuals who have experienced trauma. The story addresses the major elements that may be experienced as a result of trauma, including death, profound loss of relationship, life-altering environmental changes, feelings of guilt and self-blame, rage, powerlessness, depersonalization and derealization, loss of a sense of self, and spiritual questioning. Using the story as a reference point, participants in small groups share their own personal stories leading up to the trauma. Following along with the main character of the story, participants then share their trauma experiences. Finally, participants begin the process of finding meaning in their experiences, reconnecting with their sense of self to reestablish wholeness, and writing or telling how their story will proceed following the trauma. The model is designed to be readily implemented by human service oriented individuals within the community, such as pastors, teachers, community workers, and health workers. One need not be a professional therapist to use this curriculum. The model is a good resource for schools, churches, community organizations, therapists, or other human service workers who need resources to help people with the myriad issues caused by trauma.

If the curriculum is being used in response to a natural disaster or terrorist attack, many care providers can be trained in the model by small numbers of professionals, promoting a strong sense of "communities helping themselves" while creating a resource multiplying effect for individuals who have experienced disaster-related trauma. Using community resources allows intervention to take place immediately, and the six-session structure of the model allows the intervention to be brief, addressing the needs specific to a region or area recovering from a disaster, with a goal of preventing the development of long term trauma-related pathology.

The six sessions in the curriculum have the participants identify with a character from a story and relate their experiences to the story character's experiences. Four life stages are stressed: 1) The story of my life before the trauma; 2) My story of the traumatic event(s); 3) The story of my life since the trauma; and 4) Creating my story and defining my future. Each lesson has several activities and exercises tied to the storytelling and re-telling.

In 2010 and 2011 the model was used in Haiti after the devastating earthquake to train leaders to use the model in their communities with groups. In all, 133 pastors, 85 teachers and paraprofessionals, and 21 Community Workers were trained. The training consisted of a week-long workshop, during which the participants were first treated in small groups using the materials, followed by each individual leading a teaching demonstration of a section of the materials with a small group. The group of 85 in the teacher/paraprofessional workshop volunteered to be assessed using a pre- and post-test. There was a statistically significant decrease in post-traumatic stress scores from the participants after the treatment using the curriculum was provided. These findings are encouraging. Since the work in Haiti, groups in Newtown, CT, were trained to use the model after the Sandy Hook School shooting, and the model has been implemented in Dominican Republic, Cambodia, Vietnam, Malaysia, Costa Rica, New Zealand, and in the Middle East. While no pre and post research data was collected by these groups, anecdotal reports are equally encouraging on the efficacy of the model.

Several strong benefits of the model have emerged through the research and through use:

1) The model drastically shortens the time needed to provide treatment, from an average of 10-12 sessions for brief CBT models to a maximum of 6 sessions;

2) Due to the model's structure and ease of use and training, large numbers of volunteers can be readily trained by a small number of professionals to implement the model;

3) The need for only a few professionals to do the training provides a force multiplier in areas where professional resources are limited and the immediate need is greater than the available service;

4) The curriculum is a valuable resource for any group or individual dealing with trauma. Schools, churches, and missionary groups have used the model with great success with divorce groups, grief groups, orphanages, and trauma groups.

In addition, the model utilizes a wide range of elements from narrative and trauma research to create a program that addresses the variety of issues resulting from trauma, including the immediate shock of the trauma victim, grief and loss, the fragmentation of memory due to trauma, developing meaning from the trauma, religious/spiritual responses to trauma, and the construction of a new narrative for the victim's life (Herman, 1997; Bowlby, 1980; Stewart & Neimeyer, 2007). The following five sections review the research that supports our model and explains how and why it works.

Narrative Approaches

We live and structure our lives around our stories (Madigan, 2010). Our stories have a powerful influence over our memories, behaviors, and identities (Dingfelder, 2008). The central idea of narrative-based therapies is that people make sense of their lives and their worlds through telling stories (Stewart & Neimeyer, 2007; Schauer, Neuner, & Elbert, 2011). Trauma researchers have noted that developing a coherent narrative is vital for making sense of trauma (Briere & Scott, 2015). From a coherent narrative, the person's identity takes the form of an inner story, complete with setting, scenes, character, plot, and themes. Your life story is based on biographical facts, but it goes well beyond the facts as you use aspects of your experience and connects both past and future to construct stories that make sense to you and to your social group. This construction and reconstruction of stories helps bring memories to life and integrates memories into life to make experiences more or less meaningful (Angus & McLeod, 2004).

White's Re-authoring Model

Michael White and David Epston created narrative therapy, in its re-authoring version, in the late 1980s and early 1990s. Re-authoring has developed into a variety of psychotherapy applications and has become one of the most influential models in the narrative therapies. Re-authoring says that you correct dysfunctional psychological processes caused by trauma by the construction of new narratives of life. Trauma causes a problem-saturated narrative which becomes your dominant story and blocks you from alternative ways of thinking, feeling, acting, or behaving.

With this powerful dominant story you ignore or forget other experiences. Cognitive therapists refer to this as cognitive distortion: exaggerated or irrational thought patterns that perpetuate the effects of psychopathological states, especially depression and anxiety (Matos, Santos, Goncalves, & Martins, 2009).

Despite the recurrent and overpowering nature of the dominant story and cognitive distortions, even the most severely traumatized people, White says, experience what he called "unique outcomes" or stories from their lives that contradict the dominant (trauma) story. The identification and elaboration of unique outcomes (different story lines or narratives) help you to externalize the trauma and construct new life narratives based on the non-trauma story lines. White and Epson elaborate a number of techniques that help you understand a number of possible actions to consider in your development of a new narrative. With this model it becomes more likely for you to generate options, choose options that are aligned with your values, and engage in those actions that are more successful than the dominant trauma story. When this happens you are more likely to experience yourself as competent despite the challenges of the trauma. Through this narrative process, the traumatic event is externalized and loses its power to shape your identity as the focus shifts to a more internal locus of control with you choosing actions effective for handling the crisis. You are then in a better position to separate from the traumatic memories that had eroded your experience of self (Beaudoin, 2005).

Creation of Linguistic Representation

Another narrative type trauma treatment approach is the Creation of Linguistic Representation. A growing body of research demonstrates that post-trauma symptoms are a failure of memory;

particularly, a disruption in the conversion of sensory experience to verbal or linguistic memory. This concept is important for this curriculum and supports key concepts of narrative therapy. Historical clinical accounts from Janet in the 1880's and 90's noted the fragmented and non-linguistic quality of clients' trauma memories, and more recent study has demonstrated that traumatic memories are unique. Trauma memories are retrieved sensory fragments with no verbal component (Van der Kolk, 2014).

Kaminer (2006) further explains:

> Within this literature, the creation of linguistic representation of fragmented images and sensory experiences – that is, the development of a coherent verbal trauma narrative that names and organises the affects, cognitions, behaviours and sensory experiences associated with the trauma – is the central process of recovery for trauma survivors. (pp. 485)

Developments in neurophysiology have added another dimension to the understanding of the narrative processing disruption that identifies traumatic memories. In the brain, in memory creation and storage, the amygdala, part of the limbic system (fight or flight system), is responsible for interpreting the emotional significance of incoming sensory information. The hippocampus is responsible for integrating and organizing this sensory information and "fitting it into" pre-existing information. This process also includes the pre-frontal cortex in the frontal lobe of the brain and the thalamus in the mid-brain. When trauma occurs, due to the highly emotionally charged nature of trauma memories, you often do not include the contextual time and space that hippocampal integration would allow (Kaminer, 2006) and the normally integrated functioning of the amygdala, hippocampus, pre-frontal cortex and thalamus is disrupted, causing fragmentation in the memory and disruption of the conversion of the memory to language.

This information suggests that treatment focusing on development a coherent trauma narrative is vital to organizing fragmented sensory and emotionally charged memories into narrative linguistic memories. Developing this coherent narrative would reduce the intrusive memories and other hallmark symptoms of trauma. To do this you: 1) assist the person to gradually organize the memory fragments into sequential episodes; 2) help them identify the characters involved in the story and their actions; and 3) help them identify their emotions, sensations, and thoughts at different stages of the event (Kaminer, 2006). 4) By telling and retelling the story, combined with physical and non-verbal activities, they are able to create linguistic memory and move the memory fragments into a verbal, cohesive memory thus giving it form and meaning.

Developing an Explanatory Account

Another trauma narrative method is to develop an explanatory account. This method helps you develop a cognitively meaningful trauma account. You and the group leader or therapist collaborate to reconstruct the trauma story, introducing into the trauma narrative cognitive insights that have been missing. As discussed earlier, following a traumatic event, it is very difficult for survivors to develop a cohesive explanatory model of themselves and others that can account for the trauma. Failure to establish this cohesive account means that the trauma is unlikely to be integrated into your cognitive map of the world.

An explanatory narrative is developed through exploring your unconscious processes that influence emotions, thoughts, and behaviors. This process helps you to complete the 'plot' of your life story. The concept of developing a cohesive narrative that accounts for and explains things is key for healing.

Identification of Post-traumatic Growth

A final theme that emerges in looking at narrative methods of working with trauma is the identification of post-traumatic growth. Post-traumatic growth (PTG) refers to the positive change experienced as a result of the struggle with traumatic or highly stressful life experiences. Tedeschi & Calhoun (2004) explained that the terms trauma, crisis, and highly stressful events are often used synonymously with each other when describing this concept. They say that post-traumatic growth is "manifested in a number of ways or five 'domains of growth' including an increased appreciation of life in general, more meaningful interpersonal relationships, an increased sense of personal strength, changed priorities, and a richer existential and spiritual life" (pp. 1). Since spiritual growth is one of the domains of PTG, Shaw, Joseph, & Linley (2004) conducted a review of 11 empirical studies which examined the relationship between religion, spirituality, and PTG. The authors reported three main findings in their review: 1) studies show that religion/spirituality are usually beneficial to people in dealing with the aftermath of trauma; 2) traumatic experiences can lead to a an enrichment or deepening of religion and spirituality; and 3) positive religious coping, readiness to face existential questions, religious participation, and religious openness are typically associated with PTG. Tedeschi & Calhoun (2004) seem to suggest that it is possible that the development of a trauma narrative could either enhance or help facilitate spirituality and/or PTG. They explain that as traumatized clients experience post-traumatic growth, these changes have a mutual influence on their life narrative in general. As

31

you struggle with trauma, when you consider and include the possibility of PTG, you are enabled to develop a revised life story. Developing your individual personal life narrative directly influences PTG, and PTG directly influences developing your new life story.

How This Curriculum Works

The Process of Dealing with Trauma

Having learned the effects, results, and symptoms associated with trauma, and looked at some of the research on narrative treatment of trauma symptoms, you can now understand the process that we will use to help you recover from the traumatic experience. The process includes: learning to center yourself in your body, to calm and focus your mind, and to remain connected to your mind and body even when talking about the trauma; learning to be fully present in the here-and-now, and to remain connected with others; learning to give words to your story, and to integrate your trauma story into your life story; learning to give meaning to your trauma experience as part of your life story, and re-authoring your story with an ending of your choosing.

You can retrain your body and its fight-or-flight response by the way you breathe and move. Meditation and prayer, music and movement to music, and deep breathing and relaxation exercises are all excellent methods of retraining your arousal system. (Crawford, 2010). At the same time, body and mind connection can be achieved through mindfulness, meaning paying attention to your bodily responses, noting that they are temporary and ever-changing, and that they respond to your intentional breathing and movement. While you pay attention to your bodily responses, you can notice also how your thoughts and emotions interact, and how your thoughts and emotions are experienced in your body. This process helps you to remember or realize for the first time that you are in charge of yourself – your body and your mind.

Because this program is designed for groups, the important need for establishing connections with relationships in a supportive environment is addressed. Research has demonstrated that a support network is one of the most powerful predictors for successful resolution of trauma (Van der Kolk, 2014). Basically, we are wired for relationship. We are meant to depend on each other. This basic wiring is subverted as a result of trauma, and needs to be reestablished.

The part of your brain that lets you be aware of yourself also maintains the connection between the logical, rational brain and the emotional brain (Van der Kolk, 2014). Part of rediscovering your sense of self involves activating this part of your brain. Translating your trauma experience into language, writing to yourself to access your own inner world, drawing a memory picture while attending to the bodily and emotional responses that result, and sharing through language your inner experiences of how you are responding to the sharing of others can all help access the self-awareness seat in your brain. Having others attend in a caring and compassionate way to your story helps keep you connected to your emotional brain, and helps minimize re-traumatization through retelling.

Finally, giving meaning to your experience allows you to incorporate the trauma as part of your overarching story, and allows you to re-author the ending of your story according to your own choices and desires. Part of this process is realizing, by integrating the trauma into your life story, that you are not defined by the trauma; in other words, your personhood or nature existed before the trauma and continues to exist after the trauma. The story we use as a backdrop for the telling of your story brings this point to life.

Group Exercises and Discussion

The story of the *Gold Stone* and the following exercises and activities are designed to be used with small groups by the regular teacher, pastor, counselor, lay-counselor, or volunteer support people. If the group approach is not possible the leader may implement the program with individuals. The objectives of the story of the *Gold Stone* and the supporting activities are to help people deal with the residual effects of trauma. The difficulties they are having may range from experiencing grief, being fearful, having nightmares, being easily startled or frightened by loud or unusual noises or reporting that they want or need some help with the bad memories. Anyone reporting difficulty of this type may benefit from participation in these groups or from individual intervention using the materials.

The program is designed to last for six lessons. It is advisable to let some time elapse between lessons. Research has shown that spending longer times with these activities allows greater time for the concepts and personal implications to be reflected upon and internal changes to take place. The authors recommend spreading the lessons over a minimum of three weeks (two lessons per week) or a maximum of six weeks (one lesson per week with follow up small group activities and homework between lessons).

The key to presenting this program is to actively engage the participants through drawing, speaking, writing, and other learning activities included here. When using the curriculum with children and youth, it is important to make parents and caregivers aware of the goals of this program and ways they may help. Solicit support by explaining the program to them and encouraging them to ask the participant about the story and the activities they are doing.

Overview of a Typical Lesson

Small groups work best when there are no less than six and no more than ten group members, including the leader. Arrange the group so that everyone can see and hear well. Circles or semicircles work best if the space and the layout of the meeting area allows. The circle/ semicircle allows everyone to see everyone else and group members can be encouraged to look at who is talking and listen attentively when others are talking. Each group should take a minimum of one hour and a maximum of ninety minutes. A typical lesson proceeds as follows:

Review the previous lesson. In the case of the first lesson, give an introduction and an overview. For later lessons, when reviewing, ask open-ended questions, such as "Who can tell me what we've learned so far?" or "Someone tell us what the story was about." When homework has been assigned between sessions, review and discuss the homework.

Reinforce. Ask the group if they have been thinking about what they have learned so far. Reinforce and encourage those who demonstrate that they are thinking about these lessons and who are beginning to demonstrate a better understanding of the issues associated with the traumatic events in the *Gold Stone* story or their own story.

Introduce the activities for today. Each lesson has activities associated with the lesson that have a specific objective. State the objective to the group members. For example: "Today we are going to look at *Caonaciba's* life before the traumatic event. We are also going to explore what life was like for us before our traumatic event." Instruct the group members to pay close attention to what life was like before the trauma for the story character and for each group member. Ask questions and make statements that lead to introspection, such as, "Notice what/ how you feel when…" and "What do you feel while…?" Also lead members to explore the narrative by asking, "What happens next?"

Present the section of the story. Read the part of the story, *Gold Stone*, appropriate to the lesson, pausing occasionally to ask questions and assist understanding.

Review the part of the story. Follow the questions in the lesson for that day's activities. In addition, ask the group members Who, What, When, Where, and How questions about the story to reinforce the ideas and build comprehension of the story. This reinforces the building of a cohesive narrative with a beginning, a middle, and an ending, an important piece of resolving their own trauma.

Summarize. Review the main points of the part of the story you covered today, and tie those back to the main points of previous sections of the story. Be sure to highlight succinctly all the main points you have covered in all the lessons.

Transition to the activity. Introduce the activity which reinforces the concept for today.

Wrap up. Complete the activity, then bring the group together to review, highlight, and reinforce the ideas and concepts covered by the activity, and to discuss the relationship of the activity to the concepts.

Preview. Tell the group what the lesson will be next time and let them know that you will be observing to see who is learning and applying the ideas and concepts of the lessons. Encourage the group members to talk with their loved ones (family members, friends, or support systems) about the story and the lessons. Assign any homework that is prescribed by that section of the materials.

After the lesson, think through how the lesson went, what the strengths and weaknesses were, how to improve the next lesson and ways you can demonstrate the concepts for the group members. Between and during lessons, if possible, monitor the group members closely for any trauma symptoms, reinforce those who seem to be managing well, and encourage those who may still be having some difficulty.

Keep the *Gold Stone* book and CD available for the group to use as necessary. Some group members may wish to re-read the book on their own or listen to the CD on their own. You will use this story as a reference point to complete the exercises for the remaining group meetings.

Lesson I: Introduction and Overview

Supplies needed: The book *Gold Stone*, Paper (butcher paper, sketch pads, printer paper, etc.), crayons, colored pencils, or colored markers, music player, soothing and rhythmic music selections.

The leader greets each group member and introduces him/herself. Then each member introduces him/herself. The leader then explains the purpose of the group and what will be happening for the next six meetings.

Have everyone stand up, remaining in the circle. Play soft, slow, and rhythmic instrumental music in the background during the exercise. Ask the members to breathe deeply, concentrating on how their body feels as the air enters their lungs, and then how their body feels as the air leaves their lungs. Have members focus on breathing as deeply and slowly as possible; next, ask them to focus on their exhale, taking a pause for a beat after each exhale. Once again, ask members to notice how their body feels, suggesting they check in on each part of their body. Explain the purpose of the exercise to members by saying, "We are going to notice our breathing today, because if we are feeling our breaths entering and leaving our bodies, we are connected to our bodies in the here-and-now, because we can breathe in the present but we cannot breathe in the past or future." Take just a few moments and allow anyone who wants to share how this exercise felt to share.

Divide the group into dyads, and give each member a piece of butcher paper long enough for them to lie down on and a set of markers to share. Have each dyad take turns drawing an outline around each other on their butcher paper. Then ask the members to draw on their "body" outline where they feel their feelings. They can use different colors and different symbols to represent the feelings, or simply draw how it feels to them and where each feeling is located. For members that struggle with identifying feelings or locating those feelings in their body, remind them of the breathing exercise and suggest they begin with how they felt after the deep breathing. Suggest they explore the basic emotions of happy, sad, mad, and scared, if they struggle to name any feelings. Instruct the dyads to share their drawings with each other once both have finished the exercise. For each area of the body identified in the drawing, have the partners ask each other, "If that part of your body could speak, what would it say?" Once the sharing is complete, instruct members to ask each other to notice how their bodies are feeling now, and to share any differences they sense than when they started the exercise. Then allow any members who would like to share with the whole group to share their drawings. (Kaduson and Schaefer, 2003).

After the introduction and initial body awareness exercises, the leader reads the book *Gold Stone* aloud to the group. After reading the story, the leader asks Who, What, When, Where, and How questions to make sure the group members understand the story and can report back the significant characters, events, ideas, and concepts.

Next ask the group to draw their favorite character or event in the story, share it with a partner, and explain why they like that person or event most. In order to build group cohesion, it is a good idea to have members pair up with someone new rather than remaining in the initial dyad;

however, if someone expresses discomfort with changing partners, be flexible and allow members to operate within their comfort level.

Ask for volunteers to share with the whole class.

After the sharing and discussion, as time allows in the first session, tell the group you want them to make two more drawings. The first is called **"This is Me: I Am…"** and it is their self-portrait. It should be a picture of how they see themselves. Once again, members can use symbolic representations. Encourage those who feel insecure with their drawings that as long as the picture expresses their feelings and internal view of themselves, and they feel connected to it, then the drawing is exactly what it needs to be. The second is "**My Space**." This drawing shows how they see their world, their position in it, and their reaction to it. Use the following questions to guide the exercise. Do you believe you have a space in your world? What are you relationships with significant others? Where do your fears, wishes, anger, depression, and personal strengths and weakness fit in? How do you tolerate your world in the present? Do you feel isolated and withdrawn or included and part of the world around you? (Spring 1993). Once again, encourage those members who feel uncomfortable with art that the exercise is for their benefit, and it only matters how they view the questions and how they represent their own feelings on the paper.

After each drawing, discuss the drawings and what they mean to the members. If time does not allow for completing this exercise during the first session, assign the two drawings as homework, then have the discussion on the two drawings at the start of the next session.

Lesson II: Life before the Trauma

Supplies needed: The book *Gold Stone,* music player, soothing and rhythmic music selections

Greet everyone and ask if there are any questions before getting started. Once questions have been addressed tell the group that for this meeting you will be looking at life before the trauma. Tell them you hope that everyone will feel comfortable enough to share their own story.

Have the group retell the story of *Gold Stone.* Listen carefully and ask questions to reinforce the concepts, themes, and main ideas of the story and to make sure they sequence the story correctly, with a beginning, a middle, and an ending. Prompt members with questions such as, "And then what happened?" or "What happened next in the story?" Encourage as many group members as possible to contribute to the retelling of the story.

Pre-Trauma History and Personal Identity

Exercise: Read Part I of the story (pages 1-9) and have the group reflect on Caonaciba's life before the trauma. Ask and discuss the following questions:

Who was he?

What was his life like?

What were some of his beliefs?

What were some of his values?

What was his reality?

How are you like Caonaciba?

Reflect on your life before your traumatic event:

Who were you?

What was your life like?

What were your beliefs?

What were your values?

What was your reality?

Have each person share their reflections and have the group discuss them. Be kind and supportive and require all the group members to listen attentively and support the other members as they share. Reinforce appropriate behavior and thank each person as they share by letting them know that you understand how hard it can be to talk about difficult personal things.

Once everyone has had the chance to share their reflections, have everyone stand and complete the deep breathing exercise again. Play soft, slow, and rhythmic music in the background. This time, as they are breathing, add simple movements. Remind members to continue to notice their breathing, to focus on exhaling and pausing before inhaling again, and to notice how each part of their body feels. The simple movements can be swaying gently, or lifting their arms with their palms facing each other from their sides to above their heads and stretching toward the sky, or extending their arms out to the sides with palms down, or spreading their feet apart slightly and shifting their weight from foot to foot in rhythm with the music. Make sure during their movements that they are still feeling their breaths enter and leave their bodies, and are keeping their breathing slow, deep, and steady. Check in with members and allow them to share how this exercise felt. Ask them to compare their feelings during this exercise with the last breathing exercise. Finally, point out how their feelings within their body change with each movement, and ask them to notice the changes.

Additional activities: If supplies are readily available and time allows, once the breathing and movement exercise is complete, have three stations set up in the room: 1) a plastic tray half-filled with art sand, play sand, or kinetic sand; 2) a plastic sheet with a lump or two of clay; and/or 3) a can of shaving cream and paper towels or cloths. If these supplies are not available, go directly to the homework. If they are available, divide the group into dyads, and allow the dyads to take turns at each of the stations. The instruction for each station is to immerse their hands in the material and notice how it feels against their skin. For the sand, run your fingers through the sand and move the sand around in the tray. For the clay, knead the clay and form it and shape it with your hands. For the shaving cream, spread shaving cream on your hands and massage it with your fingers into your hands and (if comfortable) arms. Have the dyads share with each other what they notice about how the material feels against their skin and how their bodies react to the touch of the materials. Remind members to keep their breathing slow and deep as they work with the materials. Once everyone has had the opportunity to experience each of the materials, check in with members and allow anyone to share with the whole group who would like to share.

Once the breathing (or additional materials) exercise is completed, share the following homework exercise for them to complete before the next meeting.

Homework: Have each person write or draw or tell their story of life before the trauma. Tell them they will share the story of their life before the trauma for the next lesson. Encourage the group members to work on their story with their loved ones (family members, friends, or support systems) at home.

Lesson III: The Traumatic Event

Supplies needed: the book *Gold Stone*, your pre-prepared butterfly, cardboard, construction paper, tape, notebook or printer paper, crayons, colored pencils, markers, pens, pencils, music player, soothing and rhythmic music selections

Greet everyone and ask if there are any questions before getting started. Once questions have been addressed ask each person to share their homework by reading aloud, sharing their drawing, or telling their story of life before the trauma. After processing the homework, ask the group to review the previous portions of the story by asking, "Who can share with me what has happened in the story so far?" After a brief review, begin this lesson.

The Trauma and its Effect

Exercise: Read and reflect on Part II (pages 11-15) of Caonaciba's story - his trauma

What happened?

How do you think he felt?

How did his life change?

What happened to his beliefs?

What happened to his values?

What happened to his reality?

How are you like Caonaciba?

Reflect on the trauma:

What happened?

How did you feel?

How did life change?

What happened to your beliefs?

What happened to your values?

What happened to your reality?

Have each person share their reflections and have the group discuss them. Be kind and supportive and require all the members to listen attentively and support the others as they share. Reinforce appropriate behavior and thank each person as they share by letting them know that you understand how hard it can be to talk about difficult personal things. Then transition into the following large group activity:

Exercise: The Message (modified from an activity first presented by Cindy A. Stear, in Kaduson and Schaefer, 2003). Before the activity begins, the group leader creates a large colorful butterfly from available materials such as construction paper and cardboard. Tape the butterfly on the wall in the room. To begin the activity, the leader shares that one of the difficult things that happens when we lose someone is that we feel we do not have the chance to say goodbye, or to say other things to our loved ones that we wanted to say. Explain to the group that the butterfly represents new life, since it begins life as a caterpillar, then it goes into a cocoon (which is like death) and is reborn out of the cocoon as a new and beautiful butterfly.

The teacher continues, "So, we are going to use this butterfly to carry a message to any loved ones that we have lost." Have the group members draw pictures, write poems, write letters, or create their own way to communicate their message for their loved ones. While they are creating their messages, play soft, slow, and rhythmic music in the background. If some members are unable to verbalize what they want to say, or if they seem to struggle with expressing these feelings, the leader can suggest that they draw a picture of themselves doing their favorite activity with their loved ones, or draw a picture that represents their feelings they are having about their loss. Once the messages are completed, have the group members tape the drawing or writing onto the butterfly. Inform the group that the butterfly will take their messages to their loved ones that evening. Ask the group what they believe their loved ones will say in response to their messages. Ask members to notice how their bodies feel as they share. Once everyone who wants to share has done so, allow the group to create a solemn ceremony to signify the messages are ready and to prepare the butterfly to go on its way. After the group ends and the members have gone home, the leader removes the butterfly from the room so the next meeting day the group members may notice that it is gone.

Once the exercise is completed, share the following homework exercise for them to complete before the next meeting.

Homework: Have each person write or draw or tell their story of their traumatic experience. Tell them they will share the story of their experience for the next lesson. Encourage the members to do this assignment with their loved ones (family members, friends, or support system).

Lesson IV: Life after the Trauma

Supplies needed: the book *Gold Stone*, notebook or printer paper, crayons, colored pencils, markers, pens, pencils, music player, soothing and rhythmic music selections

Greet everyone and ask if there are any questions before getting started. Once questions have been addressed ask each person to share their homework by reading aloud, sharing their drawing, or telling their story of their trauma. Notice anyone who is able to connect with feelings as they tell their trauma story, and allow ample time for the expression and sharing of those feelings, as members are able to share. If they are unable to find language to share the feelings, provide paper and crayons or markers, and suggest they draw out those feelings for themselves. Ask them to focus on where the feelings are occurring in their bodies. Encourage and reinforce the decision to share their trauma experience with others. Once everyone has had opportunity to share and discuss the homework, ask the group to review the previous portions of the story by asking, "Who can share with me what has happened in the story so far?" After a brief review, begin this lesson.

Life after the Trauma and its Impact on My Story

Exercise: Read and reflect on Part III (pages 17-21) of Caonaciba's story-what happened after the traumatic event?

What happened?

49

What was his life like after the trauma?

What happened to his beliefs?

What happened to his values?

What was his reality now?

How are you like Caonaciba?

Reflect on your life since the trauma:

What is happening now?

How do you feel?

What is life like for you now?

What happened to your beliefs?

What happened to your values?

What is your reality now?

Have each person share their reflections and have the group discuss them. Be kind and supportive and require all the members to listen attentively and support the others as they share. Reinforce appropriate behavior and thank each person as they share by letting them know that you understand how hard it can be to talk about difficult personal things. Once everyone has had the opportunity to share, transition to the following activity.

Activity: The Rhythm of Life

Begin by playing slow, soothing, rhythmic instrumental music. Have members stand and do the deep breathing exercise they have practiced during previous lessons. After about five slow, deep breaths, ask members to notice the rhythm of the music that is playing. Then ask members to begin tapping along with the music's rhythm. They may tap lightly against their legs, gently clap their hands together, or gently tap with their fingers against their chest. Remind members to continue to pay attention to their breathing as they tap with the rhythm of the music, noticing each breath as it enters and leaves their body. Pay attention to any members who are having difficulty with finding the rhythm of the music, and encourage and assist them as needed. Instruct members that the goal is not to make loud noise with their tapping or clapping, but to gently synchronize themselves with the rhythm of the music. Ask them to notice how their bodies feel as they get in tune with the music's rhythms. Once the activity is completed, discuss and allow members to share how they felt during the activity. Then, as time allows, transition to the next exercise.

Exercise: **My Life's Road.** Have members draw a timeline of their lives, including significant events, and any things that have shaped their lives. Encourage members to be creative in how they express these events and how they choose to create their unique personal timeline. Play slow, soft, and rhythmic music in the background as members are working on the exercise.

Ask for volunteers to share their drawing. Discuss the drawings and what they mean.

Once the exercise is completed, share the following homework exercise for them to complete before the next meeting.

Homework: Have each person write or draw or tell their story of life after the trauma. Tell them they will share the story of their life since the trauma for the next lesson. Encourage the group members to do this assignment with their loved ones (family members, friends, or support system).

Lesson V: Defining Life From Now On

Supplies needed: the book *Gold Stone*, music player, soft rhythmic music selections, paper, pens, pencils, crayons, colored markers or pencils

Greet everyone and ask if there are any questions before getting started. Once questions have been addressed ask each person to share their homework by reading aloud or telling their story of life after the trauma. Notice anyone who is able to connect with feelings as they tell their story of life after the trauma, and allow ample time for the expression and sharing of those feelings, as members are able to share. If they are unable to find language to share the feelings, provide paper and crayons or markers, and suggest they draw out those feelings for themselves. Ask them to focus on where the feelings are occurring in their bodies. Encourage and reinforce the decision to share the experience with others. Once everyone has had opportunity to share and discuss the homework, begin this lesson.

Exercise: The Pot of Gold at the End of the Rainbow (modified from an activity first presented by Karen Hutchison, in Kaduson and Schaefer, 2003). The group leader begins by playing some calm, soothing, relaxing music. Lead the group members in the deep breathing exercise from previous meetings. Have members close their eyes as they practice their deep breathing. Once the group members have taken several long, slow, deep breaths as they listen to the soothing music, give these instructions: "Imagine you are sitting looking out your window. Outside the window is the aftermath of your traumatic experience. What do you see? Draw for me whatever you see when you are looking out your window." Keep the music playing throughout the drawing activity. Once everyone is finished with their drawing, ask if anyone would like to share what they have drawn. Some members may choose not to share, which is perfectly fine. Others may express some emotions as they share. Encourage their expression of feelings with your calm and soothing, slow-paced responses. Pay attention to members who may be shutting down or avoiding their feelings, and those who may be overwhelmed by their feelings, and encourage them to continue breathing deeply and focusing on where in their bodies their feelings are expressed. When this part of the activity is over, continue with these instructions: "Now, close your eyes again, and imagine that it is gently raining outside your window. (If you have some music that includes the sounds of rain, you can play that music during this part of the activity). Watch how the rain washes and cleanses everything. See how the land takes in the water and how the plants get greener and begin growing because of the refreshing rain. Now look up into the sky, and watch as the clouds part and the sun comes out from behind the clouds. Look! A rainbow is forming, coming down out of the sky until it touches the ground. Look at all the beautiful colors of the rainbow. Now open your eyes and draw the rainbow that you saw outside your window." As the group members are drawing, continue to play the soothing music. Once the drawings are completed, the group leader can comment on the drawings, how beautiful the rainbows are, etc. The leader then talks about how legend says that every rainbow has a pot of gold at the end of it. Tell the group members it is like a special treasure that signals the end of the storm. Ask them what they believe will be in their pot of gold at the end of their rainbow. Allow each person to share, if they choose to do so. End the activity by having them draw their individual treasure that they imagine is in their pot of gold. Encourage them to take their drawings home with them, reinforcing that the pot of gold is their special treasure that means the storm has ended. Always encourage and remind members to notice what is going on within their bodies at all times. Explain to them how paying attention to what is going on within them helps to connect them to their feelings and reconnect their memories to their bodies, which aids in healing.

Once the exercise is completed and everyone has had the opportunity to share, ask the group to review the previous portions of the story by asking, "Who can share with me what has happened in the story so far?" After a brief review, begin this exercise.

My Life From Now On: I Get to Write my Own Story

Exercise: Read and reflect on Part IV (pages 23-24) of Caonaciba's story - what defined his life?

What happened in this last part of his story?

What was his life like in the last part?

What happened to his beliefs?

What happened to his values?

What was his reality now?

How are you like Caonaciba?

Reflect on defining your life from now on:

What are you going to do?

How do you feel?

Is the trauma going to define the rest of your life or are you going to define the rest of your life?

What happens now to your beliefs?

What happens now to your values?

What is your reality going to be?

Have each person share their reflections and have the group discuss them. Be kind and supportive and require all the group members to listen attentively and support the others as they share. Reinforce appropriate behavior and thank each person as they share by letting them know that you understand how hard it can be to talk about difficult personal things.

Once the exercise is completed, share the following homework exercise for them to complete before the next meeting.

Homework: The leader explains how some people allow a traumatic event to determine how their lives will be from then on, and how some people choose for themselves how their lives will be in spite of the trauma. Remind them how Caonaciba learned to choose his own course for his life. Have each person write or draw or tell how they will define their lives from now on. Tell them they will share their homework for the next lesson. Encourage them to do this assignment with their loved ones (family members, friends, or support system).

Lesson VI: Review and Evaluation

Supplies needed: paper, pens, pencils, crayons, colored markers or pencils, music player, soothing and rhythmic music selections

Greet everyone and ask if there are any questions before getting started. Once questions have been addressed ask each person to share their homework by reading aloud or telling how they will define their lives from now on. Notice anyone who is able to connect with feelings as they tell their story of how they will define their lives from now on, and allow ample time for the expression and sharing of those feelings, as members are able to share. If they are unable to find language to share the feelings, provide paper and crayons or markers, and suggest they draw out those feelings for themselves. Ask them to focus on where the feelings are occurring in their bodies. For those who worked on the homework with loved ones, reinforce the decision to share the experience with others. Once everyone has had opportunity to share and discuss the homework, begin this lesson.

Exercise: The Diamond in the Dirt

Begin by reminding members how Caonaciba's namesake was the Gold Stone, which defined him before the trauma, but after the trauma he lost connection with his true self and his true name. Through the help of his guides, Caonaciba was able to reconnect with his true self and reclaim his true name. Then share the following: "Like Caonaciba, you have a true identity; a true "name" that defines you. Just like a diamond, when it is out in the sunlight, uniquely captures and reflects light and colors of the rainbow, your identity reflects your inner beauty and everything that makes you unique and one-of-a-kind. Sometimes, though, diamonds get covered up by dirt that is piled up on them over time. "Dirt" represents traumatic circumstances that happen to us and beliefs we come to have about ourselves as a result of those hurts from our past. The dirt might hide the diamond and the dirt might keep the diamond from shining with its unique color and light, but it does not change the diamond, because the diamond is much stronger than the dirt. In order for the diamond to once again shine, you simply brush the dirt off of it and bring it back out into the light. And that is what we are going to do in this activity." Instruct each member to write one word in the center of a piece of paper that they believe in the deepest part of their hearts is true of them. This word can be anything they choose, but encourage the members to make the word some part of their nature. Some examples they might choose include words such as "caring" or "survivor" or "sensitive" or "strong-willed" or "determined." Have each member share their unique word and discuss it briefly. Then for each word shared, ask the group to call out words that they know are true of people who are described by that word. For example, if someone chooses the word, "sensitive," the group might call out, "loving, quiet, calm, giving, easily hurt, compassionate, warm." Have the member write all of the words called out on their paper in a circle around their central word. Complete this exercise for each member. Once everyone has created a composite of all of the descriptors shared for them, inform the members that this paper is their "diamond;" that it is unique and one-of-a-kind; and, most importantly, it is not defined by the trauma. Allow members to discuss how it feels to see themselves in this way, as described by those words. Have the members take their "diamond" page home to keep, to remind them who they are.

Once everyone has had ample opportunity to share, continue to the following exercise.

Additional activity: As time allows, and if materials are available, place several magazines of different kinds around for each member, as well as scissors and glue. Ask members to cut out pictures to create a collage that represents their "diamond" (who they truly are), using pictures they cut out from the magazines. Allow members to share their collages and discuss them with each other. If these resources are not available, transition to the next exercise.

Exercise: Drawings

Re-do some of the drawings from previous meetings. Play soft, soothing, rhythmic music as they complete the drawings, and remind members to breathe deeply and slowly and pay attention to their breathing as they draw. Compare to the first set of drawings to give members an idea of the progress they have made.

1. **This is Me: I am...** This drawing shows you what you think about yourself. It is your self-portrait.

2. **My Space.** This drawing shows how you see your world, your position in it, and your reaction to it. Do you believe you have a space in your world? What are you relationships with significant others? Where do your fears, wishes, anger, depression, and personal strengths and weakness fit in? How do you tolerate your world in the present? Do you feel isolated and withdrawn or included and part of the world around you?

Discuss the similarities and differences in each of these drawings with those drawings made earlier. Allow members to process their views on how they have grown and changed through their experiences. In any ways that members see positive growth and changes, reinforce that changes are constant and are possible, remembering that trauma survivors often feel "frozen" or "stuck" in the trauma.

After each drawing, ask who wants to share and discuss the drawings and what they mean.

Wrap up by asking if there are any other questions or comments. Thank everyone for participating in the group. Remind them that they now have the ability to decide how their life moves forward. Unfortunately, bad things happen in life but they are not defined by those events. Explain how they are now equipped to deal with trauma, difficult times, and adversity as it happens by applying the things they have learned and experienced. Leave them with this encouragement: Remember these lessons and choose to write a meaningful story.

Bibliography

American Psychiatric Association. (1994). *Diagnostic and Statistical Manual of Mental Disorders,* 4th ed. Washington, D.C.: American Psychiatric Association.

Angus, L. E., & McLeod, J. (2004). *The handbook of narrative and psychotherapy: Practice, theory, and research.* Thousand Oaks, CA: Sage Publications, Inc.

Baker, G.R., and M. Salston. (1993). *Management of Intrusion and Arousal Symptoms in PTSD.* San Diego: Association for Traumatic Stress Specialists (International Association for Trauma Counselors).

Beaudoin, M. N. (2005). Agency and Choice in the Face of Trauma: A Narrative Therapy Map. *Journal of Systemic Therapies, 24*(4), 32-50. doi: 10.1521/jsyt.2005.24.4.32

Bowlby, J. (1980). *Attachment and loss.* New York, NY: Basic Books.

Briere, J. N., & Scott, C. (2015). *Principles of trauma therapy: A guide to symptoms, evaluation, and treatment* (2nd ed.). Los Angeles, CA: Sage.

Cattanach, A. (2008). Working creatively with children and their families after trauma: The storied life. In C. A. Malchiodi (Ed.), *Creative interventions with traumatized children.* (pp. 211-224). New York, NY: Guilford Press.

Colson, Denise A. (2004). *Stop Treating Symptoms and Start Resolving Trauma: Inside-Out Healing for Survivors of All Types.* Author House, Bloomington, IN

Crawford, Allison (2010). *If "the body keeps the score': Mapping the dissociated body in trauma narrative, intervention, and theory.* University of Toronto Quarterly Vol 79, 2.

Crossley, M. L. (2000). *Introducing narrative psychology: Self, trauma and the construction of meaning.* Maidenhead, BRK England: Open University Press.

Dingfelder, S. F. (2011). Our stories, ourselves. *American Psychological Association: Monitor Staff*, 42.

Foa, E.B., & Rothbaum, B. O. (1998). *Treating the trauma of rape: Cognitive-behavioral therapy for PTSD.* New York: Guilford.

Herman, Judith L. (1997). *Trauma & recovery.* New York, NY: Basic Books.

Kaduson, H. and Schaefer, C. eds. (2003). *101 Favorite Play Therapy Techniques Volume III.* Northvale, NJ: Jason Aronson Inc.

Kaminer, D. (2006). Healing processes in trauma narratives: A review. *South African Journal of Psychology, 36*(3), 481-499.

Kamya, H. (2012). The cultural universality of narrative techniques in the creation of meaning. In R. A. McMackin, E. Newman, J. M. Fogler & T. M. Keane (Eds.), *Trauma therapy in context: The science and craft of evidence-based practice.* (pp. 231-245). Washington, DC: American Psychological Association.

Langer, L. L. (1991). *Holocaust Testimonies: The Ruins of Memory.* New Haven: Yale University Press.

Leahy, R. L. (2009). Those Damn Unwanted Thoughts. *Psychology Today.*

Madigan, S. (2010). *Narrative Therapy (Theories of Psychotherapy).* Washington D.C.

Matos, M., Santos, A., Gonçalves, M., & Martins, C. (2009). Innovative moments and change in narrative therapy. *Psychotherapy Research, 19*(1), 68-80. doi: 10.1080/10503300802430657

Meichenbaum, D. (1994). *A Clinical Handbrook/Practical Therapist Manual: For Assessing and Treating Adults with Post-Traumatic Stress Disorder.* Waterloo, Ont.: Institute Press.

2000. Treating patients with PTSD: A constructive narrative approach. *Clinical Quarterly* 9(4):55, 58-59

O'Connor, M., & Elklit, A. (2008). Attachment styles, traumatic events, and PTSD: A cross-sectional investigation of adult attachment and trauma. *Attachment & Human Development, 10*(1), 59-71. doi: 10.1080/14616730701868597

Oncu, E., & Wise, A. (2010). The Effects of the 1999 Turkish Earthquake on Young Children: Analyzing Traumatized Children's Completion of Short Stories. *Child Development, 81*(4), 1161-1175. doi: 10.1111/j.1467-8624.2010.01460.x

Pack, Margaret (2008). *Back from the edge of the world: Re-authoring a story of practice with stress and trauma using Gestalt and Narrative approaches.* Journal of Systemic Therapies, Vol. 27, 3.

Pennebaker, J.W. (1997).*Opening Up: The Healing Power of Expressing Emotions.* New York: Guilford Press.

Rosenbloom, D., and M.B. Williams. (1999). *Life After Trauma: A Workbook for Healing.* New York: Guilford Press.

Rothschild, B. (2000). *The Body Remembers*: *The Psychophysiology of Trauma and Trauma Treatment.* New York: W.W. Norton.

Schauer, M., Neuner, F., & Elbert, T. (2011). *Narrative exposure therapy: A short-term treatment for traumatic stress disorders (2nd ed.).* Cambridge, MA: Hogrefe Publishing.

Shaw, A., Joseph, S., & Linley, P. A. (2005). Religion, spirituality, and post-traumatic growth: A systematic review. *Mental Health, Religion & Culture, 8*(1), 1-11. doi: 10.1080/13674670320000157981

Stewart, A. E., & Neimeyer, R. A. (2007). Emplotting the traumatic self: Narrative revision and the construction of coherence. In S. Krippner, M. Bova & L. Gray (Eds.), *Healing*

stories: The use of narrative in counseling and psychotherapy. (pp. 41-62). San Juan

Puerto Rico: Puente Publications.

Tedeschi, R. G., & Calhoun, L. G. (2004). Post-traumatic Growth: Conceptual Foundations and

Empirical Evidence. *Psychological Inquiry, 15*(1), 1-18.

Tedeschi, R. G., C. L. Park, and L. G Calhoun, eds. (1998). *Post Traumatic Growth: Positive*

Changes in the Aftermath of Crisis. Mahweh, NJ.: Lawrence Erlbaum Associates, Inc.,

Publishers.

Ursano, R. J., Grieger, T. A., & McCarroll, J. E. (2007). Prevention of post-traumatic stress

consultation, training, and early treatment. In Van der Kolk, B. A., McFarlane, A. C., &

Weisath, L. (Eds.), *Traumatic Stress: The effects of overwhelming experience on mind,*

body, and society. New York, NY: The Guilford Press.

Van der Kolk, B. A. (2014). The body keeps the score: Brain, Mind, and Body in the healing of

trauma. New York, NY: Viking.

Van der Kolk, B. A. (1999). The body keeps the score: Memory and the evolving psychobiology

of post-traumatic stress. In M. J. Horowitz (Ed.), *Essential papers on post-traumatic*

stress disorder. (pp. 301-326). New York, NY: New York University Press.

Van der Kolk, B.A. (1996). Trauma and memory. *Traumatic Stress: The effects of*

overwhelming experience on mind, body and society. New York: Guilford Press.

Van der Velden, P. G., Wong, A., Boshuizen, H. C., & Grievink, L. (2013). Persistent mental

health disturbances during the 10 years after a disaster: Four-wave longitudinal

comparative study. *Psychiatry and Clinical Neurosciences, 67*(2), 110-118. doi:

10.1111/pcn.12022

White, M. (2007). *Maps of Narrative Practice*. New York, NY: W.W. Norton & Company, Inc.

White, M., & Epston, D. (1990). *Narrative Means to Therapeutic Ends*. New York, NY: W.W. Norton & Company, Inc.

Zang, Y., Hunt, N., & Cox, T. (2013). A randomised controlled pilot study: The effectiveness of narrative exposure therapy with adult survivors of the Sichuan earthquake. *BMC Psychiatry, 13*. doi: 10.1186/1471-244X-13-41

BIOGRAPHIES

W. David Lane

W. David Lane, Ph.D., Professor, Department of Counseling and Human Sciences, Penfield College of Mercer University, is the founder of the Counseling Program and Ph.D. program at Mercer University in Atlanta. He earned the Ph.D. in Counseling from Georgia State University in 1992 and has more than thirty-nine years of experience as a counselor, counselor educator, and supervisor. David is a Licensed Professional Counselor, a Licensed Marriage and Family Therapist, a Nationally Board Certified Counselor, a Certified Professional Counselor Supervisor, and a Clinical Member of the American Association for Marriage and Family Therapists. He is in his twenty-first year at Mercer University.

He has published numerous articles, book chapters, and manuscript reviews in the field of Counseling and Marriage and Family Therapy. He is the co-author of Ready to Learn: Teaching Children How to Succeed in School, a national award-winning program for pre-school and early childhood classrooms, and Please Share the Door, I'm Freezing: Creating Oneness in Marriage, a Christian marriage workbook co-authored with his wife, Donna. He and Donna also co-authored Gold Stone, the story used as the basis for this curriculum. He is a regular presenter at local, regional, national, and international workshops in the field of counseling.

After the earthquake in Haiti in 2010, David worked extensively for over a year in Haiti leading teams of professionals to train pastors, teachers, and mental health providers in trauma assessment and care. In the wake of the Newtown, CT, Sandy Hook School shootings in 2012, David led teams to train pastors and community workers to assist with the trauma.

Donna E. Lane

Dr. Donna Lane is Assistant Professor of Counseling at Liberty University, Adjunct Professor of Counseling at Mercer University, and a Christian Counselor in private practice since 1993. She is founder of the Cody Lane Foundation, which provides individual and small group discipleship and Christian education. She has presented at local, regional, national, and international conferences and workshops on such topics as trauma, grief and loss, marriage counseling, toxic religion, early childhood education, parenting, narrative therapy, counselor education, and soul care. She participated in training workshops for pastors and community workers in Newtown, CT, following the shootings at Sandy Hook. She also co-authored the award-winning Ready to Learn series, which teaches preschoolers and elementary students needed learning skills. With her husband, David, she co-authored the Christian marriage workbook, Please Share the Door, I'm Freezing: Creating Oneness in Marriage, and Gold Stone, the story used as the basis for this curriculum. With her son, Hayden Lane, she co-authored the book, Restored Christianity, which is currently in its second edition.

Donna and David have been married thirty-six years, and have three wonderful children; Hayden, Lindsey, and Cody, who passed away in 2007 after a battle with a degenerative neurological disorder.

Do NOT WRITE IN BOOK
ANSWER QUESTIONS ON A SEPARATE PIECE OF
PAPER